Whispers Of The Heart

A Symphony of Feelings

Mathew Varghese

BookLeaf Publishing

India | USA | UK

Made with ❤ on the BookLeaf Publishing Platform
www.bookleafpub.in
www.bookleafpub.com

Dedication

To the quiet moments that spoke to my soul,
To the glances that sparked love,
To the tears that taught me strength,
And to the smiles that brought me joy.
This book is a piece of my heart.
May it touch yours.
With love and gratitude.

Preface

Every poem in this collection is a whisper from my heart, a fragment of my soul captured in words. The journey to creating this book began in moments of quiet reflection, where emotions flowed freely and thoughts took shape in the form of poetry.

The genesis of Whispers of the Heart lies in the myriad experiences that have colored my life. From the tender moments of love to the profound depths of sorrow, each emotion has left an indelible mark on my heart. These poems are my way of making sense of the world, of finding beauty in the chaos and meaning in the mundane.

Writing this book has been a deeply personal journey. It has allowed me to explore the vast landscape of my emotions, to confront my fears, and to celebrate my joys. Each poem is a piece of my heart, a testament to the resilience of the human spirit and the power of vulnerability.

I hope that as you read these poems, you find echoes of your own experiences. May they offer you comfort in times of sorrow, joy in moments of happiness, and a sense of connection in the shared human experience.

Thank you for allowing me to share these whispers with you. May they resonate with your heart as they have with mine.

Acknowledgements

Creating Whispers of the Heart has been a journey filled with emotion, reflection, and growth. I am deeply grateful to everyone who has supported me along the way.

To God, who has been the cornerstone of every blessing in my life.

To my wife Merin and my son Nathaniel for being there for me and loving me the way you guys only can.

To my mom Mary and my sisters Liz and Susan, for their unwavering love and encouragement. Your belief in me has been the foundation upon which this book stands.

To my best friends Sandy and Abhi who kept pushing me to write again, been my sounding boards and my sources of inspiration. Your insights and support have enriched my writing in countless ways. For many my poetry was a source of amusement , but you guys pushed me

To all my friends who have guided, been a part of the journey and wished the best for me

To my Jiju achachan and Nami chechi- thank you for being a blessing in my life and taking care of me like a younger brother ..

To the readers, for opening your hearts to my words. Your connection to these poems is what brings them to life.

And to the quiet moments, the fleeting glances, the tears, and the smiles that have shaped my soul. This book is a testament to the beauty of life's emotions.

Thank you for being part of this journey.

1. Abyss

It was like sitting on a butterfly
or the highest levels of intoxication
Her ruses made me take the plunge
Into the painful void of black

Not able to step forward
Not able to step backward
Stuck I was
No way to escape

Nearing the end
Her sinewy fingers
Reached out for my jugular
She pulled me into the abyss
Abyss of Death ,

2. Life is beautiful ...

The phone went blank,
And I turn back and start walking
Walking through the heap of insults,
Wondering where I had gone wrong

Trudging the lonely long road back,
Memories of her came back.
Wished to hold her once more in my arms,
Wished to whisper sweet nothings into her ear once
again.

I meet with silence all around,
A thousand around me, not one that I can call mine to be
found.
Desperately searched for her loving voice,
And wished that I could be her choice.

I reach out to hold her hand,
She pushes me away.
Nuisance I became,

Bugger, irritation, waste and what not.

For a second with her,
I wished a thousand times,
But for a lifetime without me
She wished a million times

3. Goodbye

Met her that fateful day of January,
Shrouded in black, She welcomed me
Little did I know that this chance encounter
Was one I would always remember.

Crying, I entered her life,
She wiped my tears,
Drove away my deepest fears,
And taught me how to live.

I began to trust her,
Like I'd done no other.
All I wished for was her,
And what would make me happy for a while.

Came the drought,
But no fear.
As long as she was near,
I had all to cheer.

Turning back, to call her
Found no answer.
Empty space welcomed me
There was no one I could see.

Memories of times spent flooded my mind,
Times that I thought were one of a kind.
That's all that's left me was with the gift of tears and
hope so dear.
Entangled in her web.
I want to break free.
Will do one day,
Will do one day.

4. In Pieces

I bend over,
To pick up the broken pieces
We loved, we lived, we shared
We seem so far away, nothing but a dream

What can one speak,
When words itself hurt?
How can one be quiet?
When silence kills every moment

The storms, they came,
I held onto you, felt secure
Little did I know
You were the storm itself

Waves they blew fast and furious
Taming your fury, scorching me in its wake
Yet try again to hold your hand
But you push me down again

All that is left now
Are the pieces.
Broken dreams, shattered hearts, weakened people
I bend over,
To join the broken pieces

5. Where Her Heart Resides

Her laughter fills the quiet spaces,
Warming the cold, empty places.
It's not just joy—it's a spark divine,
A sacred hymn, where heartstrings entwine.

Her eyes, twin lanterns in the dark,
Set my world alight, ignite the spark.
They hold a story both wild and kind,
A truth that leaves reason behind.

Every touch, like whispers of fire,
Echoes her soul, my one desire.
Her presence—a storm, a serene tide,
Both chaos and peace, where her heart resides.

She doesn't just walk; she flows through life,
Cutting through struggles, dull and rife.
And I stand here, caught in her wake,
A willing captive to all she creates.

Forever I'm hers, a soul unbound,
In her light, purpose is found.
Not just beauty—but a force so rare,
She is my life's answer, my one true prayer.

6. Eternal in Your Eyes

Life unfurls like a lover's embrace,
Each dawn revealing your radiant face.
Threads of gold weave our story divine,
Moments together, your heart entwined with mine.

The whispers of wind, the warmth of your smile,
Make every journey feel worthwhile.
In your arms, I find blossoms anew,
Sadness fades in the light of you.

Sorrows pass, like clouds on high,
Their shadows fleeting in love's clear sky.
Your touch, a balm, your voice, a song,
With you, life's beauty feels ever-strong.

Oh, my love, a river we share,
Its bends unknown, but with you, I dare.
For in this fragile and fleeting guise,
We find eternity in each other's eyes.

7. Threads of Connection

The world spins, a ceaseless dance,
Yet in its turning, we find a chance,
To grasp a thread, a fleeting gleam,
The shadow of a shared dream.

What ties the hearts, what binds the hands?
What bridges seas and foreign lands?
A force unseen, yet deeply felt,
In its warmth, our fears melt.

Love, not just passion's flare,
But presence, patience, the act to care.
A language spoken without sound,
In silence, a solace found.

And yet the threads are fragile, thin,
A truth that aches from deep within.
For time and space may shift the tide,
Leaving us longing for what's inside.

But let us cherish the tangled strands,
For life's richest gifts are found in bands—
In fleeting bonds, the bittersweet,
In every soul we chance to meet.

8. A Mother's Gift

Oh,Amma, my guiding light,
You stood strong through every fight.
Through storms and struggles, you held on,
So I could rise with each new dawn.

Your hands, though tired, shaped my way,
Carrying dreams to a brighter day.
You gave your all, you gave me more,
Even when your own heart felt sore.

Every tear you hid from sight,
Every sacrifice, every sleepless night
You built a future with love so deep,
Planting seeds for me to reap.

And now, as I stand tall and free,
I know it's all because of you
Thank you, Amma, for all you gave,
For your love, your strength, your endless wave.

9. The Sun Still Rises

When night unfolds in endless black,
And hope feels lost, too far to track,
The world still turns, the dawn arrives,
A golden whisper—life survives.

Through morning mist and gentle light,
The sun ascends, defies the night.
Its quiet voice, a soft embrace,
Hope is never out of place.

So even when the shadows grow,
And sorrow's tide begins to flow,
Remember—darkness never stays,
The sun still rises, warm with grace.

10. A Symphony of Moments

A rustling leaf, a sparrow's song,
The hum of earth, where life belongs.
A child's laughter, crisp and bright,
A candle flickering in the night.

The way the ocean breathes and sways,
The scent of earth in fresh-born days.
Time hums a tune, it calls, it sings,
And whispers joy in simple things.

So listen close and let life play,
A melody to guide your way,
For even in the silent air,
A symphony is always there

11. The Colors We Carry

Beyond the gray of sorrow's mist,
Beyond the aching clenched-tight fist,
Life holds colors, deep and wide,
If only we set fear aside.

The way a sunset claims the sky,
With brushstrokes bold, with flames that fly.
The way a smile can lift the air,
As kindness paints the world with care.

Not every shade is bright and clear,
Some carry pain, some cradle fear.
But even night—its ink so deep—
Holds twinkling stars we choose to keep.

So look beyond, let wonder stay,
Paint your story in your way.

12. An Ordinary Miracle

A heartbeat strong, a steady breath,
A flower rising from its death.
The way the rain revives the earth,
The simple spell of life's rebirth.

A falling star, a whispered dream,
The way the moon lets silence gleam.
A stranger's kindness, pure and true,
A life restored, the sky in view.

Not grand, not loud, but always there,
A miracle in each small prayer.
The things we miss, the things we take
They build the world that we create.

13. Spirit

In the depths of darkest night,
When hope seems far away,
A spark within begins to light,
And turns the night to day.

Through trials faced and battles fought,
The spirit stands its ground,
With every challenge, wisdom's sought,
And strength within is found.

No storm can break, no tide can drown,
The heart that dares to dream,
For in the soul, a steadfast crown,
A flame, a constant gleam.

With every fall, it rises high,
Unbowed, unbroken, free,
For resilience is the will to try,
And shape one's destiny.

So when the world seems harsh and cold,
And shadows cloud your view,
Remember, in your heart, behold,
The power to renew.

For in the face of storm and strife,
The spirit will prevail,
With resilience, you'll embrace life,
And write your own brave tale.

14. It's all about Hope

In the silence of the dawn,
When night begins to fade,
A glimmer of the light is drawn,
And darkness starts to wade.

Hope rises with the morning sun,
A promise of the new,
A whisper that the day's begun,
With skies of endless blue.

Through trials faced and shadows cast,
Hope shines a guiding light,
A beacon that will always last,
To turn the wrong to right.

In moments when the heart feels weak,
And dreams seem far away,
Hope gives the strength we often seek,
To face another day.

It's in the laughter of a child,
The bloom of spring's first flower,
In every act of kindness mild,
Hope shows its gentle power.

So,hold to hope, let it inspire,
And lift your spirit high,
For in its glow, you'll find the fire,
To reach and touch the sky.

15. The Echoes of Eternity

Eternity whispers softly,
Through the corridors of time.
Life's inspiration echoes,
In every heartbeat's chime.

In the vast expanse of forever,
Moments linger and fade.
In the echoes of eternity,
Our dreams are gently laid.

Each whisper a reminder,
Of the infinite we seek.
Inspiration's voice grows kinder,
In the silence, we speak.

The echoes of eternity,
Resonate through the ages.
Inspiration's gentle plea,
Guides us through life's stages.

In the quiet of the night,
We hear eternity's call.
Inspiration's guiding light,
Helps us rise and never fall.

Through the corridors of time,
We walk with dreams in hand.
In the echoes of eternity,
Life's inspiration stands.

16. Heart to Heart

When the road is long and winding,
And the journey seems too tough,
The heart within keeps finding,
The strength to rise above.

Through trials faced and mountains climbed,
With every step, a gain,
Perseverance, deeply primed,
Endures through joy and pain.

No storm can break, no doubt can sway,
The spirit firm and true,
For in the darkest, coldest day,
The heart knows what to do.

With grit and grace, it pushes on,
Through every twist and turn,
For in the soul, a fire is drawn,
A flame that fiercely burns.

Each setback faced, each challenge met,
Becomes a stepping stone,
With perseverance, never fret,
For you are not alone.

So hold to hope, and keep the pace,
Let courage be your guide,
For in the heart, a steadfast place,
Where dreams and strength reside.

17. The Dawn's Whisper

In the quiet hush of morning,
Life breathes its first gentle sigh.
A whisper of hope unfurling,
Underneath the vast, azure sky.

The sun peeks over the horizon,
Casting golden hues on dew-kissed leaves.
Birds sing their morning anthem,
As the world awakens and believes.

Each ray of light a promise,
Of dreams yet to be born.
Inspiration's gentle caress,
Guides us through the dawn.

The flowers stretch and yawn,
Petals glistening with morning dew.
In the dawn's embrace, we find,
A world refreshed and new.

The breeze carries whispers,
Of stories yet untold.
Inspiration's tender touch,
Turns the mundane into gold.

As shadows retreat and fade,
The day begins to bloom.
In the dawn's soft serenade,
We escape night's gloom.

18. The Dance of Dreams

Dreams pirouette in twilight's embrace,
A ballet of stars in the night.
Inspiration's tender grace,
Guides us towards the light.

Under the moon's soft glow,
Our aspirations take flight.
In the dance of dreams, we know,
The beauty of life's endless night.

Each step a story told,
Of hopes and fears entwined.
Inspiration's dance unfolds,
In the rhythm of the mind.

The stars twinkle like dancers,
In a cosmic ballet.
Dreams weave through the darkness,
Showing us the way.

In the quiet of the night,
Our hearts beat in time.
With every dream's delight,
We reach for the sublime.

The dance of dreams continues,
Through the hours of night.
Inspiration's gentle muse,
Guides us to the light.

19. The Heartbeat of Time

Time's relentless march,
Echoes through our veins.
Inspiration's spark ignites,
Breaking life's chains.

With each tick of the clock,
Moments weave a tapestry.
In the heartbeat of time, we unlock,
The secrets of eternity.

Every second a chance,
To chase the dreams we hold.
Inspiration's guiding glance,
Leads us to the bold.

The sands of time flow swiftly,
Through the hourglass of life.
In each grain, a story,
Of joy, love, and strife.

The heartbeat of time pulses,
With memories old and new.
Inspiration's light compels us,
To see our journey through.

As minutes turn to hours,
And hours turn to days,
We find strength in time's power,
Inspiration's endless ways.

20. The Flame Within

A flame flickers in the dark,
Guided by unseen hands.
Life's inspiration sparks,
Lighting dreams across lands.

In the shadows, it dances,
A beacon of hope and light.
Inspiration's flame enhances,
The beauty of the night.

Each flicker a promise,
Of dreams yet to ignite.
In the flame within, we find,
The courage to take flight.

The flame burns ever bright,
In the depths of our soul.
Inspiration's guiding light,
Makes us whole.

Through the darkest night,
The flame within persists.
Inspiration's gentle might,
In every heart exists.

As the flame grows stronger,
We find our path anew.
Inspiration's light will linger,
Guiding us through.

21. Canvas of Life

Life paints with colors bold,
On a canvas vast and wide.
Inspiration's story told,
With every brushstroke applied.

Each hue a memory,
Of joy, sorrow, and grace.
In the canvas of life, we see,
The beauty of every face.

With every stroke, a tale,
Of dreams and hopes anew.
Inspiration's vibrant trail,
Guides us through and through.

The canvas stretches endless,
A masterpiece in the making.
Inspiration's touch is boundless,
With every stroke, life is waking.

Colors blend and swirl,
Creating scenes of wonder.
In the canvas of life, we unfurl,
Dreams that pull us asunder.

Each brushstroke tells a story,
Of love, loss, and delight.
Inspiration's path to glory,
Painted in the light.

22. The Symphony of Silence

In silence, a symphony plays,
Notes of hope and despair.
Life's inspiration sways,
In the stillness of air.

The quiet hum of existence,
Speaks louder than words.
In the symphony of silence,
Our deepest thoughts are heard.

Each pause a melody,
Of dreams and fears combined.
Inspiration's harmony,
Resonates in the mind.

The silence holds a power,
A symphony so grand.
In its quiet, we discover,
Life's gentle, guiding hand.

The whispers of the wind,
The rustle of the leaves,
In the symphony of silence,
Our soul finds reprieve.

In the stillness, we listen,
To the music of the heart.
Inspiration's notes glisten,
As life's symphony starts.

www.ingramcontent.com/pod-product-compliance
Lightning Source LLC
LaVergne TN
LVHW010021200726

843495LV00015B/1869

9 789369 537891